A Guide  *ter*

A Guide
to Nature in Winter

Northeast and North Central
North America

DONALD W. STOKES

Illustrated by
Deborah Prince and the author

Little, Brown and Company

Boston – New York – Toronto – London

LIBRARY OF CONGRESS CATALOGING IN PUBLICATION DATA

Stokes, Donald W
    A guide to nature in winter.

    Bibliography: p.
    Includes index.
    1. Natural history—North America. 2. Winter—North America. 3. Nature study. I. Title.
QH102.S76   574.5'0974   76-26861
ISBN 0-316-81720-1 (hc)
ISBN 0-316-81723-6 (pb)

HC: 15   14   13   12   11   10   9   8
PB: 15   14   13   12

MV-NY

Designed by Susan Windheim
*Published simultaneously in Canada
by Little, Brown & Company (Canada) Limited*
PRINTED IN THE UNITED STATES OF AMERICA

How to Use This Book

This book contains a number of separate field guides, one for each prominent aspect of nature in winter. Each guide is divided into three parts: general information on the subject, a key for identifying the different members of the subject, and specific natural history descriptions of each of the members.

The general information will be most useful if you read it before going out, for it will most likely expand your conception of winter and sharpen your approach to seeing.

The keys are designed for simple use in the field, but becoming familiar with them ahead of time will make it easier for you to identify things when you find them.

After identifying a plant or animal, look up its name in the natural history description that follows the key; the names are in alphabetical order. These descriptions point out things to look for and enjoy in what you have found. If it is too cold to read them in the field, remember the name and read the description later in the warmth of your home.

Contents

A Guide to Nature in Winter

1

Winter Weeds

*M*OST PEOPLE THINK weeds are particularly offensive types of plant, when in reality many plants we call weeds are used in other countries as cash crops or garden ornaments. There is really no difference between plants and weeds; weeds are simply plants growing where they are not wanted.

But despite the fact that weediness is in the eye of the beholder, there are certain plants which continually grow where not wanted, and they all have at least three features in common. First, they are aggressive colonizers, either producing great quantities of seeds that are widely dispersed or having far-reaching roots which produce new shoots. Second, they grow primarily on land affected by humans, such as cleared or cultivated land, roadsides, gardens, and dumps, and in this land they can tolerate a wide range of soil and climatic conditions. And third, most of these plants, now widespread in North America, are not native to this continent, but were brought here from Europe by early settlers, either knowingly as herbs, or accidentally, as in livestock feed or in the ballast of ships.

When these plants were introduced, the northeastern quarter of North America was dominated by an established forest. The new weeds could not have survived in that damp environment of filtered light, competing with plants already well adapted. But when the settlers cleared land for towns, farms, and roads, a new environment was created, one filled with sunlight and turned-over earth. This was the aliens' previous haunt and they quickly dominated it, spreading by way of roads and paths, from town to farm and from town to town. A few native plants have learned to compete with them, but to this day the alien weeds stick close to humans, shunning the dark forest and crowding into the sunlight and often poor soil of roadsides, fields, and vacant city lots.

Some of these plants remain standing throughout winter, and these can be called winter weeds. One of the functions of these dried weeds is to disperse seeds. Two methods of seed dispersal are most common. One is by wind, as in Milkweed, where seeds are supported on the air by an attached parachute of filaments. The other is by animals, as in Burdock, where the seeds are encased by burs, which get caught in the fur of passing animals. These two methods are seen repeatedly among winter weeds, each species having its own variation on the theme.

Although most weeds in winter appear dried and lifeless, this is far from the case. Some are, indeed, completely dead except for seeds at the tips of their stalks (e.g., Wild Lettuce, Peppergrass); but others are still alive, either within the ground as strong roots (e.g., Dock, Cattail) or above as living deciduous stalks (e.g., Spiraea).

To get the most from hunting and observing winter weeds you need to be aware of all their points of interest, including their life patterns, their use by animals, their adaptations for survival, their method of seed dispersal, and of course the beauty of their colors and forms.

Not all winter weeds are included in this guide. Only those that are particularly longlasting, beautiful, or interesting appear here. These can be found in any open space, from city lots to roadsides to wild meadows. In fact, this is one aspect of nature that may be actually more diverse in the city than the country.

Key to Winter Weeds

For each winter weed there is a drawing of its silhouette and, next to it, an enlarged drawing of a portion of its flowerhead. The average height is given below the name. In order to facilitate identification, most of the drawings are grouped under headings suggesting outstanding characteristics.

WEEDS WITH THORNS OR BURS

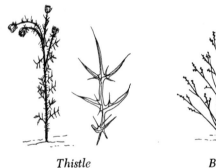 

Thistle
2–4 ft.

Burdock
3–6 ft.

WEEDS WITH TRANSLUCENT "SEEDPODS"

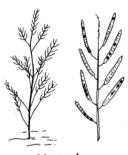 

Mustard
1–3 ft.

Peppergrass
1–2 ft.

WEEDS WITH NO BRANCHING

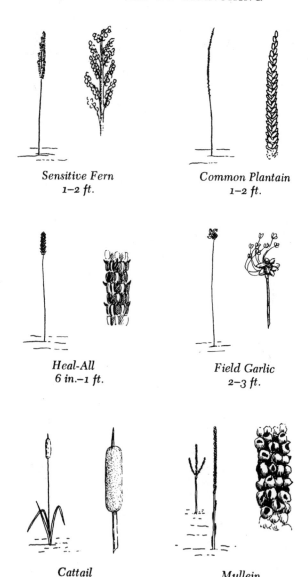

Sensitive Fern
1–2 ft.

Common Plantain
1–2 ft.

Heal-All
6 in.–1 ft.

Field Garlic
2–3 ft.

Cattail
3–4 ft.

Mullein
3–8 ft.

WEEDS WITH BRANCHING ONLY AT TOP

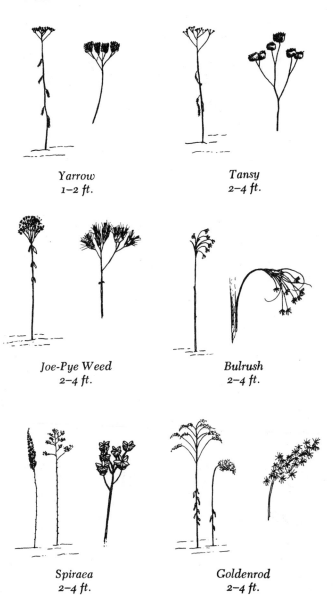

Yarrow
1–2 ft.

Tansy
2–4 ft.

Joe-Pye Weed
2–4 ft.

Bulrush
2–4 ft.

Spiraea
2–4 ft.

Goldenrod
2–4 ft.

WEEDS WITH OPPOSED BRANCHING

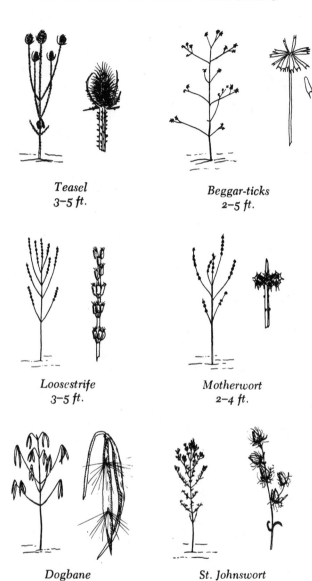

Teasel
3–5 ft.

Beggar-ticks
2–5 ft.

Loosestrife
3–5 ft.

Motherwort
2–4 ft.

Dogbane
1–3 ft.

St. Johnswort
1–2 ft.

WEEDS WITH SPARSE BRANCHING ALONG THE STEM

Aster
1–2 ft.

Black-eyed Susan
1–3 ft.

Chicory
2–3 ft.

Wild Carrot
2–3 ft.

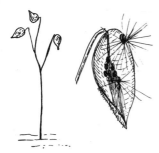

Milkweed
2–4 ft.

Evening Primrose
2–4 ft.

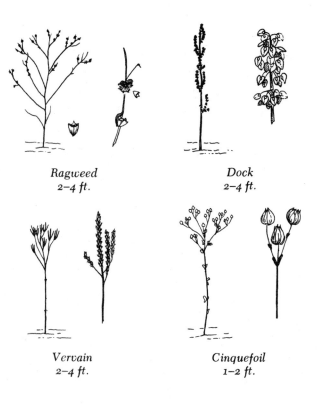

Ragweed
2–4 ft.

Dock
2–4 ft.

Vervain
2–4 ft.

Cinquefoil
1–2 ft.

Natural History Descriptions

Asters (*Aster* species)

Asters are typically the flowers of fall. Their name, which means "star," is derived either from their bright petaled blossoms or the star-shaped pattern of their tiny winter flowerheads. These dried flower parts are similar to those of Goldenrod, another winter weed, and reveal the close relationship between the two plants.

Aster

Both are members of the famous family of Composites, considered one of the most modern and successful products of plant evolution. Instead of producing large petals to attract insects, Composite flowers are individually small and inconspicuous, but they grow in groups, forming a showy mass. The plant conserves energy by producing fewer petals. And it is more efficient for pollination, for one insect can pollinate hundreds of tiny flowers in a single visit.

There are over 250 species of Asters, some of which last as winter weeds. Asters are perennials and their underground roots remain for many years, producing new flowers each fall. So, having found Asters once, you will know where to find them again, both in winter as a dried stalk and in the next fall as a blossoming plant.

Beggar-ticks (*Bidens* species)

It is likely that Beggar-ticks will find you before you find them. After a winter walk through lowland fields you can expect your socks, pants, or coat to be covered with its small seeds. The Latin name of the genus means "having two teeth," but knowing Latin won't help avoid the consequences. Each seed is covered with a hard coat which has at least two barbs covered with backward-directed hairs like the points of a harpoon. The seeds are arranged on the winter stalk with these barbs projecting outward. Since the seeds are loosely attached, the slightest contact with fur or clothes insures their transportation to a new area. Beggar-ticks are annuals, and must be replanted every year. So each plant you find is from a seed carried and dropped in that place last year.

From left to right, seeds are: Beggar-ticks, Spanish Needles, Swamp Beggar-ticks, Leafy-bracted Beggar-ticks

The plant favors moist ground, as found in swamps or ditches. Its large, bright yellow summer flower, a welcome addition to these unused wet areas, has earned it the additional name of Brook Sunflower.

Its other common names are more descriptive of its winter habits: Spanish Needles, Sticktights, Bur-Marigold.

There are a number of species of *Bidens* in North America. Each has a slightly different seed shape or number of attached barbs, but all are the same in their habits. Next time you get stuck with Beggar-ticks you might as well relax and enjoy it. Pluck out a seed, compare it with the ones shown here, and see what kind has found you.

Black-eyed Susan

Black-eyed Susan (*Rudbeckia* species)

The flower of Black-eyed Susan is truly the "day's eye" (the original meaning of Daisy) of summer meadows, a black center surrounded by bright yellow petals staring up from among the grasses. But in winter only a few clues lead us to a remembrance of that summer quality, and one is the black-eyed center, now a marvelous design of matured seeds. The seeds are arranged in spirals, descending both clockwise and counterclockwise from the top of the cone. Their crisscrossing geometry is somehow startling, reminding us that the mathematics of our minds has long been present in nature.

Hard to distinguish from Black-eyed Susan in winter is its close relative, Coneflower, so named because of its dark

Black-eyed Susan
flowerhead

cone-shaped center. Both plants belong to the genus *Rud-beckia*, a name given by Linnaeus in honor of his botany professor, Olaf Rudbeck (1660–1740), a man who also once wrote a book claiming Sweden to be the site of the lost Atlantis.

The species named for Black-eyed Susan, *Hirta*, means hairy, and refers to hairs that cover the leaves and stem. They probably protect the plant from losing too much water through evaporation.

Black-eyed Susan is a biennial, forming just a rosette the first year. It loves to grow in hot sunny fields and is a native of our midwestern plains. As more and more people migrated to the Midwest and roads were cut through the wilderness, Black-eyed Susans moved east. Now in the East and South they are a common sight, enlivening fields and roadsides with their sunny presence.

Bulrush (*Scirpus* species)

The Bulrushes form a large group of similarly shaped grasses. A number of them are conspicuous in winter, and

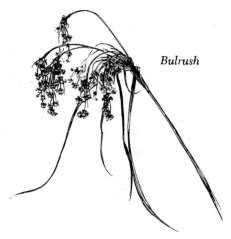

Bulrush

their lone stalks, topped with a fountain of flower parts and seeds, will be found by even the most casual winter weed collector. They are picturesque plants and make a fine addition to any winter weed arrangement. They always grow near water — sometimes in it, sometimes at its edge, sometimes set back in a marshy area. In this moist soft earth they easily extend their rootstalks, which in turn send up new shoots.

Bulrushes are extremely valuable to wildlife. Waterfowl feast on the dark seeds; Muskrats enjoy the rootstalks. They also provide cover for nesting birds and young mammals.

Most Bulrushes are distinguished from other grasses by their triangular stems, but those most often found as winter weeds have round stems. Other common names for members of the genus *Scirpus* are Woolgrass and Threesquare.

Burdock (*Arctium* species)

Finding your clothes studded with Burdock's burs can be an irritating discovery. But it is also a chance to learn at first hand about the animal dispersion of the plant's seeds. You have obviously been chosen as a likely volunteer to perform the job.

The efficiency of Burdock's seed dispersal is due to the structural design of the bur. Its outside is covered with

Burdock bur

small recurved hooks, which easily penetrate fur or clothing but, once in, hold the bur tight. Attached to the hooks are sheaths, which enclose the seeds. When an animal pulls on the bur the hooks lock, so that the sheaths separate, thus releasing the seeds. The fact that Burdock is a native of Europe and Asia, and now widespread in North America, is proof enough of the success of its method.

Burdock is a biennial. It takes two years to flower and produce seeds, completing its life cycle. In the first year it is

Burdock first-year rosette

a rosette of foot-long leaves; during the second summer it grows a tall stalk with pink flowers which later in the fall form burs.

There are two main species of Burdock in North America: Great Burdock (*Arctium lappa*), which grows a stalk up to ten feet tall, and Common Burdock (*Arctium minus*), which grows to only half that height.

At the end of the first year's growth, Burdock's large tap-root qualifies as an edible winter vegetable; it has also been harvested commercially for medicinal purposes. The second-year summer stalk is also edible when peeled and boiled. As food for wildlife, however, Burdock is seldom used, because the seeds are well protected by burs, the stem is lined with

Burdock

tough fibers, and the large leaves contain an extremely bitter juice.

Cattails (*Typha* species)

Cattails are a sign of an environment in transition, for they are a key plant in changing wet areas into dry land.

Cattails

Growing in the shallows of ponds and swamps, their starchy rootstocks form a thick mat just under the water surface. Each year as old stalks die back, new shoots grow from the root stalks. In a few years the marshy area around the roots may become covered with decaying matter from earlier growth. This creates soil where once there was water. Plants that prefer this moist earth move in, crowding out the Cattails. Meanwhile, the Cattails produce new shoots, farther out in open water. In this way Cattails and their companion plants continually encroach upon the open water of ponds and swamps.

This succession can be slowed by the presence of Muskrats, which use Cattails for all aspects of their lives. They eat the shoots in spring, the leaves and stems in summer, the roots throughout the fall and winter. Besides using the dense stands as protective cover, they use the stalks and leaves to construct their water homes. Cattails also provide protective cover for nesting wildfowl.

Cattail flowerhead

The brown, cigar-shaped flowerheads topping the tall stems contain up to 125,000 seeds per head, surrounded by packed fluffy matter. All through winter these flowerheads continue to break apart, looking like the stuffing from leaks in old chairs, while wind and water carry the seeds to new muddy areas of the shoreline. In winter the fluff is used by mice to insulate their homes, and in spring it will be used by birds in the lining of their nests.

Cattails are easily seen while driving, for they grow well in the moist drainage ditches that line highways, their rigid stalks and velvet brown seeds firm against the winter wind, lasting until midsummer.

Chicory (*Cichorium intybus*)

Look for the fine grooves that run the length of Chicory's winter stalk, giving it a delicate tooled appearance when viewed from close up. The flowerheads that were bright blue and daisylike in summer, now dry, hug the main stems in groups of two's and three's. Inside some of them you will see the flat ends of wedge-shaped seeds arranged in a circular pattern. If none are visible, then the seeds have been shaken out already by the wind.

Chicory flowerheads

Chicory stalk

On the lower stem are remains of Chicory's small leaves. A second type of leaf grows at the base in summer and is

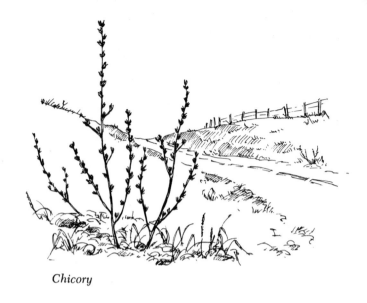

Chicory

the reason for Chicory's fame. Both Chicory and its cousin Endive (*Cichorium endiva*) grow scallop-edged basal leaves that for centuries have been used as salad greens. Even more of a delicacy are the blanched leaves of Chicory. To grow these you must dig out the roots in fall, bury them in a box of soil, and place them in a dark warm area. With watering, the roots produce white or light yellow leaves which make a crisp addition to any salad. This accounts for one of Chicory's common names, Witloof, or "white leaf."

In the southern United States and many countries of Europe, Chicory is grown as a commercial crop for its long taproots. When roasted and ground up, these make a strong additive to, and sometimes a hardy substitute for, coffee.

Chicory is a native of Europe, brought to North America by European immigrants who were accustomed to using it. It is a perennial and thus takes a few years to become well-established; nevertheless, it is extremely common. It is found in the neglected edges of parks, sidewalks, and roadsides.

Cinquefoil (*Potentilla* species)

Cinquefoil is a weed that is common in open areas with poor soil. It rarely grows more than knee-high and has lovely open branching. At the tips of each branch there are cup-shaped flowerheads, which now loosely contain numerous small seeds. As you knock the plant in passing, the seeds are shaken out through the open edges of the cups.

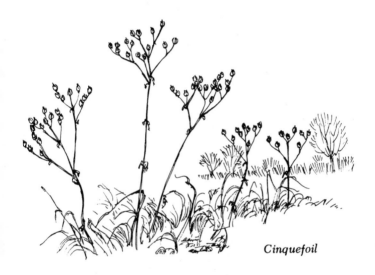

Cinquefoil

There are many species of Cinquefoil, some low-lying plants, others erect and shrubby. The one most often found in winter is Rough-fruited Cinquefoil. Like other Cinquefoils, it sends out leafy runners across barren ground. At various points these runners send down roots and produce a

Cinquefoil flowerheads

vertical stalk. The stalk dies back in winter, but very often the runner remains green. This system of vegetative reproduction is similar to that of rootstocks but occurs above the ground and is thus well suited to colonizing rocky impenetrable soil.

Cinquefoil in summer

The common name, Cinquefoil, means "five leaves" and describes the five serrated palmate leaves. They resemble a miniaturized version of the leaves of Horse-chestnut. The generic name is derived from the Latin word for "powerful"; it was given in the belief that Cinquefoils were valuable as an astringent medicine. There seems to be no present evidence of this healing power, although the roots of some species are edible, and a tea can be made from the leaves of another.

Common Plantain (*Plantago major*)

To get a close look at Common Plantain, bring a stalk inside, for it's too delicate a job for gloved hands or numbed

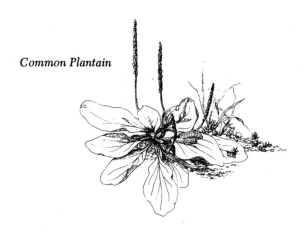

Common Plantain

fingers. You may find Plantain in your own backyard, or along a well-worn path through a field, but never where the vegetation is tall or thick, for it cannot compete with other weeds. It does best where other plants are cut back regularly, as in a yard; one of its common names is Dooryard Plantain.

Another common name for it is Rattail, which describes its long pointed stalk coated with seed capsules at the tip. Look closely at the capsules and see the tiny cap that covers each one. You can gently pull this capsule off the stalk and break it into two perfect halves, thus releasing the seeds. There are about fifteen seeds in each capsule and hundreds

Common Plantain flowerhead

of capsules on each stalk. The seeds, being slightly sticky, are dispersed by birds and mammals.

When the seed germinates in spring it grows into a rosette of large, rounded, dark green leaves. In the second year, the plant produces the stalk with seeds, and since it is a perennial, it produces seeds each year thereafter. The seeds are eaten by birds and mice; rabbits favor the leaves and stalks. Some species of Plantain can be used as spring greens, and the dried leaves of others make a fine tea.

Although not particularly beautiful, Common Plantain has a likable character all its own, being the only winter weed that is so slender, pointed, and unbranched, reaching from the edges of park paths and growing peacefully at the base of the back doorstep.

Dock (*Rumex* species)

Dock is one of the most striking winter weeds to be found; its rich red-brown color, its spiked clusters of seeds, its gently curving stem, all combine to give it an air of abundance and vitality in the winter landscape.

It is a member of the Buckwheat Family and has the

Dock

Dock seeds   *Dock winter rosette*

characteristic triangular seed. Each seed is enclosed by three heart-shaped leaves folded in upon it. The seeds have a faint but pleasant taste and have been used to make flour, but it is more work than the taste is worth. Dock has evolved protective coatings around its seeds, so when they are eaten by some animals, they are not digested but dispersed in the animal's feces. This is a common property of many weed seeds and an important mode of dispersal.

Dock is a perennial, sending up new leaves each fall in the form of a rosette. These can be gathered in winter by digging through the snow at the base of the winter stalk. They are long lance-shaped leaves which, when boiled and seasoned with butter and salt, make a fine vegetable, rich in vitamins C and A. Some prefer Dock to our cultivated spinach.

In the loose soil of your garden, Dock can grow a taproot up to six feet long, and if you cut off the leaves this root just sends up new shoots. So the way you view Dock just depends on your state of mind; it can be either a tenacious weed or a source of healthful food and winter beauty.

Dogbane (*Apocynum* species)

Immediately conspicuous on Dogbane are its silk-para-chuted seeds, smaller than those of Milkweed, yet clearly similar to them. Its pencil-thin pods grow in pairs off the plant and split down their inner seams to release seeds. All parts of the plant are thin and gangly, so that it has a slightly untidy appearance.

Dogbane flowerhead and seeds

If you peel the reddish bark from the branches or stem you will find it tough. It was used by American Indians to make twine, and the plant's common name, Indian Hemp, reflects this custom.

The summer leaves of Dogbane have long been known to be poisonous (the word *bane* means poison or death), and, interestingly enough, tropical members of the same genus also contain potent poisons. Many of these poisons are used on the tips of arrows and spears, enabling hunters to capture game more efficiently. But there is nothing to fear of our Dogbane in winter; there are only its color and form to enjoy and its silken seeds to release in the wind.